Some Odd Afternoon

Sally Ashton

To Tree –

Some Odd Afternoon

with admiration

Sally Ashton

Sally Ashton

July 2010

BlazeVOX [books]

Buffalo, New York

Book design by Geoffrey Gatza
Cover art by Chris Roberts-Antieau http://www.chrisroberts-antieau.com

First Edition
ISBN: 9781935402817
Library of Congress Control Number 2009910034

BlazeVOX [books]
303 Bedford Ave
Buffalo, NY 14216

Editor@blazevox.org

publisher of weird little books

BlazeVOX [books]

blazevox.org

2   4   6   8   0   9   7   5   3   1

B   X

Acknowledgements

The author gratefully acknowledges prior publication of some of the poems in this book in the following: *5am, Another Chicago Magazine, Caesura, Dos Passos Review, Failbetter, Linebreak, Poet Lore, Scapegoat Review, Sentence: a Journal of Prose Poetics,* and *These Metallic Days,* Mainstreet Rag, 2005.

Special thanks to:

Nils Peterson, Marjorie Manwaring, Kelsea Habecker, Mary Donnelly, Nin Andrews, David Lehman, Brian Clements, Brad Hallum, Frank Bassett, the guys in Vancouver, and Erika Lutzner. But chiefly mostly Frank Ashton.

for Lorin, Susannah, James

Some Odd Afternoon

Some Odd Afternoon

Our lives are Swiss—
So still—so Cool—
Till some odd afternoon…

from #80 by Emily Dickinson

Prologue

Portent

The definite. An old woman knits.
The needles click and slip, specific bones
of a lifetime knotted over with joy
or looped with sorrow—every dropped stitch.

Miracles fall from the needles
which is to say too much. Far better
to suggest a simple woolen sock,
the durable effort. An unedited
sock, this version of life,
an old woman with needles akimbo.

From her hand stitches
plied knit upon purl in circular pattern
silent as yarn. Her lips move
as if in supplication, eyes saucering
toward something unbound.

from *Woman Knitting* by Chaim Soutine, Norton Simon, Los Angeles

What To Do With a Cello

Some Odd Afternoon

Emily Dickinson is dreaming of Italy. She is asleep. No she isn't, Italy rises there just beyond the window, the rooftops, the horizon. A place to look with eyes closed and open again. The Baedeker stowed in a trunk that gathers dust under the bed. Nothing packed. All the usual chores undone. So she writes something on a scrap of paper she's saved in a pocket, seeing the way some people can see. She will escape her sad country. So would a sudden flock of crows that crosses the winter sky over the barren tips of the trees and over the end of the year and another day. Gloved clouds beckon. Beyond the albino Alps, Italy awaits. She slips the paper back in her pocket—land in sight.

Christic

Christ returned, there in the middle of 6th Avenue at West 54th in front of the New York Hilton. She stood in the intersection, right in traffic, and tried to flag down a taxi. God decided to send the daughter this time. She stood with her arm raised, unperturbed by the rush of cars on either side or the cacophony of horns that blared rapid-fire. No one stopped. I passed her on my way to O'Briens' and almost said *Christ, get out of the street, are you crazy or something*, but it wasn't my business and maybe she was for all I knew. I guess it was some sort of miracle. She had that let me kiss you where it hurts look on her face but she was headed the wrong direction and I had friends waiting for me. No one seemed to recognize her, or care if they did, and no way a cab was going to stop right there in the middle of traffic. *Christ*— I thought. From the pub I heard a fresh blast of horns when the light changed. I hoped she got where she needed to go and had somewhere to sleep that night, someone expecting her. And I was honestly glad to think she'd come back. Lately, things had been feeling pretty messed up. Perched on a stool with my pals I lifted a glass to her and thought, *well, get busy then*, downed my drink and for a moment it was as if I was skating, December in Central Park, one of the only people on the ice, snow just beginning to spin.

Stateside: American Mayhem

—poem in 3 voices

I'm pumping gas into my car.
I'm under my parasol watching
the first battle of the Civil War.

I'm the passenger in a four-seater plane
flying at or below 6500 feet.
We have a relative speed. Look away

for several minutes and the landscape changes
completely. Home is somewhere out there
beyond the tents, the gathered cannon.

The battle draws nearer.
I've embedded my laptop under my hoop-skirt.
It's tricky to access the keyboard,

email improbable. My opera glasses fail—
I don't need them at this proximity.
Someone brought a dog, but pity the poor horses!

Whose idea was the picnic, the champagne?
It seemed a good one before the actual shooting,
before the bleeding began. Preposterous this

bleeding, a carnival of carnage. I shift my skirt
to cover my ankles, sniff a violet sachet.
Out the window seared grasses and tiny trees,

a geometry striped green, gold,
yellow. Grandpa hides his tobacco
behind the outhouse; the slaves have run off.

I'd like to send a message, a goddamn email.
I'm encumbered by my parasol;
I can barely breathe in this fucking corset.

Ants advance across the blanket. I need
a large legal pad to continue this
piece about the war. I'll record it

in my journal and mail a copy to my sister.
I'll learn to knit socks. I'll pray.
The pilot radios air traffic control.

Houses laid in precise mosaic
form a labyrinth when you pass overhead.
A burst of static, a voice dictates numbers.

A burst of gunfire, the air singed acrid
with smoke. The noise won't stop
even when I cover my ears, even if I scream.

I want off this battlefield but my car
won't start. It's impossible to walk far
wearing a hoop skirt. I can't carry

the parasol *and* my laptop. I need to meet
a Confederate hero, interview his mother.
My mind always freezes during landing

until the wheels skid on the runway; we taxi
and my thoughts return. If a horse gets shot
they shoot it again. I get back in the buggy

and lay on the whip. I hope to get home in time
for supper. My lover joined the army.
A pigeon brings me his letters, *love Johnny.*

I keep them under my pillow, I store them
on my zip drive. I hear they shoot runaways—
slaves, horse thieves, the soldiers.

I understand the predicament, a need
for black and white photos,
but I couldn't pull the trigger.

The pilot turns off the engine, the propeller
slows to a standstill. I return the nozzle
to the pump. The battle rages.

I wouldn't send my sons, Confederacy
of my genetic material. First I'd take out
their kneecaps with a shovel; I'd put them

in hoop skirts, or on the next plane, hide them
with Grandpa's tobacco. I write
Dear Johnny, don't fuck with my narrative

clip the message to the pigeon's leg, open
an upstairs window. The bird soars free,
a contrail of feathers. I hit "send."

Winter will be cruel. Perhaps the fighting
will be finished. Snow in the trenches,
newspaper stuffed in my goddam boot.

Bear Sightings

I don't live on a street where bears rummage through mailboxes, literate bears looking for something with their name on it or at least smart bears who know mailboxes often hold samples of, say, *Kellog's Special K with Red Berries*, or sometimes a tiny tube of toothpaste which bears have a proven taste for or else you can no longer trust US Forest Service warnings, if you ever did. I live far from that street, and far from the streets where bears bully garbage cans, and from the streets hedged in blackberry bramble that beckon the bears in summer with a steaming scent of sugar. I don't live near the berry bushes that scramble away from roads into gullies and up hillsides to the dark wood where bears could be supposed to live. Back through the woods and time and memory when bears were enchanted men trapped in hide and claw and tooth, bears with large asses and moist tender snouts who fought kingdoms of bees for one pawful of honey, and villages of ordinary men for their rightful place—the throne, the love of a woman—until at last the bears became unspellbound, dis-enchanted, and took back their human skins. They live now as men, far from the dark wood and blackberry briars vined along roads they build themselves, lined with their own houses and mailboxes and one night a week cans of refuse. That's the street I live on. No trace of bears, not even a rumor.

Clocks Without Faces

Let someone else tell the time, I can't see it anymore and unlearn its courtesies, begin to dismantle its many faces, crude symbols of the realm time really occupies. Clock hands sweep flat circles, but time's true hands gesture both away and toward us at untamed angles and velocities. Holding us in the present, spinning us seamlessly away. The sundial's simplicity proves somewhat accurate, tracing time with light and the movement of shadow, as does an hourglass in its passages of sand, random grains pouring chamber to chamber, or a year marked by a revolution of the whole tipping planet. The way night like the past can be measured by dreams, or the present in the flight of a green parrot: so also the future. In this way we might move easily through time without any regulating gears if we could only remember how. And such is childhood's privilege, and such is the pleasure and the sorrow of old age.

Once, You Let a Man

Once, you let a man
you thought you would become
crawl into bed beside me.

I said speak.

He wanted me to touch
the riven face,
his cheek. I traveled
willingly past worn flesh in search
of your dark eye.

He wanted

to lie like this, spoons
against me but
you leapt up, transformed,
a wolf who swallowed
the other whole
to lie with me yourself

fur marrying skin.

Blood, bone, tooth, yes, claw,
your breath a wilderness running
across my throat.

Snowfall

The furnace knows something. The thermostat on the wall registers complaints. Snow cloud blots out the sky one shade darker than the ground. I can't write by snowlight and covet lamps, cushions, must build a fire, this house the animal I live inside like some kind of parasite worked in to its intestines most unwilling to leave. In the driveway the car waits while the snow begins to bury it. It submerges with grace. Snow takes all. Yesterday's footprints forget themselves, the way out disappears. Now dark patches under the trees whiten, age before my eyes. Snow falls faster than the trees can release so they gather winter in armfuls instead, convinced of the necessity. I continue to fall through whiteness that says beautiful, beautiful and in this can't be measured. The path to the woodpile unshovels itself while summer plays on another screen in shades of sepia out on the porch. The snow doesn't fall, the ecstatic earth rushes to meet it, or the sky falls like the drift of the galaxy and I have no shoes for this only somewhere my mother's blue boots. Somewhere. I probably gave them away. Too bad the toboggan lies in the gully, the world filling itself with snow.

I wait for a rogue wave

I wait for a rogue wave to hit or a seagull to shit in my hair, what it means to sit on a rock near unprecedented sea, the sea that sounds like itself and nothing else in the world at the edge of the world where the waves change themselves against cliff. Here comes another woman down the same path, silent because of the self-sounding sea. *Who* isn't obvious, only where and when. She hops the stream that barely troubles the surf. Next I look, she sits naked on the sand with a flame between her legs. This sounds like sex but it's pages she burns, not self or passion though that's implied. I can't bear to watch nor should I. Watch. One who waits for birdshit must not interfere with one who self-emoliates. Instead I pocket two stones, one smooth, one jagged like an arrowhead and climb back up the cliff careful at each pitched step.

And look back where one at a time each page torn out goes up in flame, each page a prayer. I don't pray, such unbinding the loosening of thought, an unbodiment of desire. *How* is a mystery and why can't be spoken. Even *what* fools the eye. Only fuel, smoke rising in a pillar, my lips flecked with salt.

Strange Hour

Strange hour, a stranger on foot.
There are roses in the corners of your mouth, at other times coarse hairs.
Love, I choose petals.

The midwife comes in.

She sharpens a knife, runs the blade through the white heat of a flame.
I take my feet out of the stirrups and get off my back.
Far better to stand, I understand.

I've been here before and want no part of the unforgettable and sweet smell
        of blood blooming on the sheet.
I'm a bleeder and don't know how to stop.
I can't suffer a sequel.

Anyway, the floor is packed dirt.
The room smells of clove and burnt toast but I'm not hungry.
I will never forgive this night, crickets on their knees crying *mercy, mercí, mercy,*
        mercí—oh wrap me in arms that want for something.

Litany

In the fall, ducks.
We have so little to go on—
the need for clowns, their sorrow

dressed up to help us somehow
endure. In the fall
ducks tattoo their flight overhead

saying, saying. What *are* the signs
of wonder? We move through the house
from cellar to attic

in a counter-clockwise direction
as if we could unwind time.
As if. In the fall

ducks crack the evening's silence.
They sound morning's
first cry, look up—

nothing insignificant in the fall.
Clowns make me weep.
We have so little to go on.

There Came Great Light

She understood darkness to be the absence of light. Day began with sunrise and woke up all that mattered to her. She lived her life in light and passed through darkness asleep. It was something of a shock when she thought to consider the opposite possibility, light a temporary stay, the day more about displacing reality than returning it to her. Dark the constant, light artificial. She felt as if she were on a planetary amusement ride, swung briefly in and back out again, the mechanism invisible to her, the ride's duration unknown.

The Map

She loved that he called her earthling, how she felt utterly alien yet most human in that same instant. A commotion in the leaves, unseasonable rain and there, something tongue-like pressed at the base of her skull. Chaotic heat. So many eyes. At first she resisted, but his persistence dismantled her one visit at a time. He traveled her speech and gesture, discovered and memorized her in contours, the ridges and rises, the hollows, until he laid claim to the country of her, each province, the waterways.

At his last visit he brought her the map he had fashioned. It shimmered like mercury and pulsed. *You keep it* she said and watched him roll it back up before he disappeared forever, but she doesn't have to see him to know how often he unfurls it, tracing, retracing.

What To Do With a Cello

Stand on a street corner waiting for the bus that takes you both home.

Lock the door; what you do with the windows and curtains is up to you.

Open the cello's case, inhale the aroma, rosin and polish, and that certain shut-up smell.

Lift the cello by the neck with your other hand around its waist.

It is like a waist, isn't it.

Clutch it between your thighs, hunch over, make the strings quiver.

Pluck it, pizzicato.

Finger furiously, sawing with the bow, elbows raised, eyebrows furrowed.

Your left hand slides up and down the strings; you are not thinking about this.

Do not miss one single note and do not stop.

Music streams from both your bellies, everyone who hears looks up.

What does it mean to end? Which vibrato, or whose?

Perhaps you will never put the cello in its case again.

When you're very old strap it across your back, get on your bike, pedal into the black and white distances.

It's always like this when the cellos come in.

What You Want

I hope you'll write fiction someday, you said
as if poetry was the literary equivalent of clitoral
orgasm or premature ejaculation
and if I only concentrated harder I'd get the hang
of it, the full bang
for my buck, I'd make it, money
up the wazoo, achieve a commercial-sized
climax, spew a torrent of words
instead of this self-absorbed stroking
of individual syllables, my god you
could go blind and I could scream you wouldn't
quite say when you did say what you did
about the fictions I should someday write.

Human Ballistics

"They were shooting each other out of the cannon in the backyard."
– Actor Paul Reubens who grew up down the street from the
Zacchini family

At their house no one knew whose turn it was to be shot from the cannon. The youngest could expect certain privileges which also identified him an easy target, a test dummy used to perfect cannon angle, velocity. In time one became accustomed to the sudden blast, tinnitus that lasted days, the smell of scorched hair, bright spots dancing—an eyebrow vanished. Not like firing a gun. They used different sets of calculations.

Airborne in an arc seeking maximum acceleration, the streak upward a perfect human parabola in spandex. Imagine for one boundless & electric moment a different outcome where gravity loses and the body defies the net's roped arms, keeps right on going, no resistance, climbing until all earth drops away.

But difficult the slide down the barrel tipped crouched waiting in darkness each breath fouled by sulfur. How harsh the striking of each match.

Two Ripenings

Why should she worry about death which didn't seem much of a mystery, like falling asleep where you never noticed when you did or that you were, only upon awakening could you say, "Oh, I slept after all," but with death there was likely no waking, and if there were wouldn't it be like beginning to dream? You could never tell when or how you did that either so you'd probably never even know you'd died whereas life, living was a mystery worth thinking about.

Like Rock

Once I heard a woman being murdered, stabbed to death blocks away, screaming and screaming for help that did not arrive. In time. I was great with child. I was awakened to her from the distance of night and dream, from an edge, from my own wifery. I lay and listened, uneven cries, wondering, knowing only sound, not sense. Just as I thought to wake my husband, all screams stopped, the California night full only of itself, familiar blanket. I too dropped to sleep. Somewhere a woman wails, yelling and moaning as if giving birth to rock. Another screams as if crushed between rock teeth. One woman cries in ecstasy, another births a child. Somewhere this is happening. Some will know, some will wish they didn't.

On Chickens

I suck a chicken bone and think of flight.

Modern chickens are bred for the largest possible breast—western man's favorite portion—and therefore cannot walk, let alone fly.

Give me liberty or give me eggs.

A chicken might be a rooster but a rooster is never a chicken.

A chicken is always fowl.

Chickens can be hypnotized; they are fervent practitioners of magic and voodoo sacrifice.

When it hatches, a chick will follow the first thing that moves. This is called imprinting and can get the chicken in a lot of trouble if its mother isn't around. See above.

Once you've plucked a chicken you will never forget.

Many things are said to be as scarce as chicken's teeth including money, hope, and hard-workers.

Another reason chickens can't fly is that farmers clip out their flight feathers and the barnyard birds forget they ever could. Like that glass wall in the aquarium experiment.

A chicken that escapes is called "Lucky." What does it escape to?

A chicken that has laid an egg is as proud as the pope, strutting in her cape of white feathers, little red cap cocked to one side.

When cooked, the chicken's tail is called the pope's nose.

I once had a chicken who decided to roost in the barbeque. Every morning she laid one egg on the grill.

Truth is stranger than fiction; chickens are stranger than truth.

A content chicken utters a "caucaucaucau" sound.

Such are the profound silences from which animals speak.

We travel by cloud

That way there is no going back. That way there are days when no progress can be made, no mileage, no points earned. That way weather takes on a whole new urgency, whether we stay or go all predicated on the atmospheric pileage of aggregate moisture condensation. All dependent on the muscle and movement of cloud.

Take this one blue day. You can't go anywhere! What a relief. Or a cloudscaped afternoon. Look at the choices that hover above. Imagine what voyages await.

For most trips I prefer kidney-shaped formations. Give me something substantive, though when it comes to cloud-travel shapes serve really about the same. But a certain comfort can be found in the kidney, the bulk and breadth, the leading outer edge, the suggestive inner curve. Fulsome. One feels, especially one new to considerations of cloud, one feels more willing to surrender to such a familiar, home-grown organ, a profundity less apparent in say cirrus, the more striate forms.

Yes, make mine kidney any day. I'm not saying I wouldn't accept a ride with another, less ovoid shape, something less accumulated. Sometimes a herd of horses appears to streak across morning, manes thinning behind. One would be more than foolish not to take advantage of that opportunity. Mount up while you can, clouds being what they are. Once I ended up with a flock of flying donkeys; it pays to keep careful watch. Donkeys aren't horses, for one thing, and with minor atmospheric shifts can be driven to unrecognizable frenzy. No, you can't get too comfortable.

Far safer kidney-style. Perhaps a slower go, but much less apt to disappear beneath you, leave you like an ass—

In the Museum

Look through an ordinary doorway and the universe expands.

—The effect of mirrors, an echo chamber, the camera obscura: to see the cosmos in miniature.

You discover chambers within chambers, a room within a room.

—How sometimes you long for other worlds.

Remove the figure from the painting and you free the imagination.

—A mediation, oil on canvas.

You then confront background with a negative space.

—Like gazing through a keyhole, something more lies just out of range.

Vision adores an aperture.

Curator of the Objects of Terrible Memory

newspaper headline

"She" is the first surprise. Next,
there is no actual museum, *Memory being*
she says, *most often the shape of a barn,*

the same timber. She hands me her card,
"Your invitation to the Tragic Kingdom."
I feel the slight motions of a plane mid-air.

Inside the barn the only light filters
through cracks between dry boards.
Something inhabits the rafters.

She climbs a ladder to the hayloft.
Something up here in a hat box
you might like to see, she calls.

It's the canning jars I'd like to avoid,
produce preserved from some ancient harvest
lined up like lab specimens across a dusty shelf.

She sits down at a polished piano and opens the lid.
Who knew she could play, too! The children
grin and sing along, eyes shining.

I can't name the tune, can't recall
what movie this scene is from. Even if I did
remember, I never get titles right.

Now she wears a uniform, pushes a beverage cart.
Something to drink? A packet of pretzels placed
on my tray-table. I pretend to sleep,

they've cut the movie so much
I can't bear to watch it anyway.
She reaches to lower the window shade.

So we arrive in China, painted land of drenched air,
temple incense. She wears embroidered silk,
raises her parasol, steps into a waiting rickshaw.

I can't make out her words over the roar of the plane
but she pats the seat beside her. I shake my head.
She motions to her driver, the credits roll,

the memory of her face already fading
the way daylight blinds you momentarily
when you leave the darkness of a barn.

Iron

one

And so began the age of iron. The sky too full of blue. Birdsong tore at the surface stillness. I sat on my bed all day feeling the weight. Outside, children's laughter rose like balloons to my window. I tried to catch them. My arms wouldn't move having already turned to iron.

two

And so began the age of iron. Silver and gold littered the streets. Even the sky grew gray and sullen. One small girl stopped to pick up a handful of coins. Her mother ignored this, shuffled through them as if they were so many dead leaves. The girl filled her pockets with bright pieces anyway. She had yet to learn the meaning of the age.

three

And so began the age of iron. Until that time men and women worked together. They followed the seasons, the berries, the deer. Now men forged blades, guns, and plowshares for their fields. Women lugged pots and kettles into new houses held together by nails. The men fashioned locks for the doors. Behind them their women polished bright spoons.

Listen

The grandfathers come for a visit. They've traveled far, their boots caked with mud. I let them sit in the living room where they shell peanuts, smoke, and laugh together, rough-handed men, mostly farmers. One sits cross-legged on the floor, another as stiff as an old tintype.

It's like a forest in there, one of them a log, another stone, one a river. One old beetle lies on his back waving great legs with feeling. I don't get everything they're saying, echoes in murmured cascade, cataracts of memory, the ancient language of trees. They'd go on forever if you let them and leave me to sweep up peanut shells and ash. Oh, those grandfathers, whispering, winking, full of magic (one pulls a quarter from my ear, another steals my nose). They speak with the voices of their mothers. Listen—ghosts attend us all.

In which I google sally ashton

Chile, when I was a girl guess I'd ruther dance dan eat.
                                        Sally Ashton, 1845

I've Got a Secret

. . . brought to you by Miracle Whip. Miracle Whip won't melt on top of your salad.

There are many ways to find yourself. Two roads diverge . . . give your dizzy head a shake, undergrowth being; what: how it went. After some years I try a google search. Whom should I find. Who? A-mazed. Mees. So manyselves. So many Sallies. We are very busy everywhere. Swarmy. We are writers, we are dancers, face bookers and face lickers. Many are British and one of us—a slave, likely owned by an ex-pat Brit. We all assume. Names, and some someness the way everyone has or will. I am here to say Sally Ashton is up for grabs, whether you marry in or assume. Or name the baby! We seem chiefly cheery sorts who'd rather dance. At least in retrospect. Don't ask Sally Ashton to look too far back, memory being what memory does. You know what it is. What it does. What slavery is. The Sally Ashtons have made do. Some of us are dead. Others, Youngsters! God bless us. Sally Ashton lives. That has made the difference. All. We are like the brave sun rising each day with miles to go, and miles to go. *My* name is Sally Ashton . . . will the *real* Sally Ashton please stand up?

Sally Ashton. Controller.

Fiction writer and student of creative writing. Surfs. Draws. Likes her privacy; likes watching, but enjoys being watched. From a distance. Blondely sitting astride her surfboard waiting for the next wave. This is the comfortable distance. The rocking motion. Not what earth provides, only here suspended above an almost abyss, an abyss stretched also above. Behind, the surface of vastness reaches around the world and back. Underneath: Aquatic. Tangy. Each wave races her back to shore where gravel rolls under her heels. She resists, paddles back out to the place between worlds, her vortex, where she is many things. Seal-like in her wetsuit she almost belongs to the breakers. Masters them atop her board, presses in to shore, thrusts forward, boardward, backward whilst she waits, whilst she runs to greet the lens, whilst she recedes like seaweed to bob and wait again. Under the black rubber skin, look, the birthmark, a bruise. *Not a sound came from her mouth. Her thin shoulders. Exposed nubs of spine . . .*

Facebook Sally Ashton

To see, be seen. To seek. To know? There she is, Sally Ashton on Facebook, and there will be more than this one, ponytailed brunette licking her friend. On the cheek, or being licked. This is about what turns up. About hits and visits and friends collected. About the users. We rise and fall in the search, its engines and desperation. The sifting of data. We fill an electronic void, an invisible cosmos of human design. Maybe a new form of consciousness? At first humans faltered before the seen world. Then our navigations drew us toward the unseen. Baffled. Now we track a universe expanded beyond stars and planets tilting in traceable paths. The measurable distances bounded by perpetually opening emptiness impossible to fill. Cosmos to chaos. Now we upload infinite variations on a finite screen. Now we grasp the application. Or not. We will say mass digitization and know what it means. We say hypertext and plain text and that too has changed. I hit the space bar, I right-click the mouse. Sally Ashton, where are you? This screen a telescope that searches the faces, assesses the preferences. Fuck privacy. What am I looking for? I am encoded. I can go no further. I have not been invited to join myself.

Finding

I was looking in a box.

I was looking into the ocean beneath a wave.

I was looking under a magic carpet.

I was looking down a mountain's throat.

I stood with my toes over the chalk line all the way.

I slept with my hair tied in a pony tail, my teeth in a jar.

I awoke, my fingertips dipped in a can of paint.

I was looking in a dirty sock.

I was looking in a dirty book.

I found a strange green place swaying beneath the waves, a sandy-bottomed room.

I stood up in the boat to look out the window.

I saw a friendly face through the watery glass and waved.

I curled up inside a barrel.

I was looking through closed eyelids.

I sat with my feet up, my hair down, a ring on my thumb.

I waited to know the answer.

I stood in the boat to see better. There! a seagull tilts in a chalky sky.

I was looking in a swimming pool where leaves float at the surface but some betray the bottom.

I fell in the subway station; how can I explain.

I believed it all came down to words I can't translate.

I believed it all came down to circumcision.

I believed.

What could I believe?

I was looking; I didn't want to say it again.

Sally Ashton (b. ca. 1845) Keswick, Va.

Interviewer: Susie R. C. Byrd
Date of Interview: Unknown (1934 I found) Albermarle County?
Source: *Negro in Virginia*, published version, p. 91

"We use to git back in de end cabin an' sing an' dance by de fiddle till day break. Sho' had one time, swingin' dem one piece dresses back an' foth, an' de boys crackin' dey coat-tails in de wind. Nobody ever bothered us, not even de patterollers, cause Marsa won't gwine let 'em. Ole fiddle was a man named Louis Crane. Chile, he sho' could strung dat fiddle. Never did so much work, but Marsa use to keep him, 'cause he use to have him play fo' de balls in de big house. Marse use to pay him too. We never did pay him, 'cause we ain't never had nothin'. But he use to play an' call de figgers 'long as dere was anyone on de floor. Chile, when I was a girl guess I'd ruther dance dan eat."

The Unbearable Ashton-ness Being

A lie. Completely invented (*Find Your Family Crest* companies: please take note). I wasn't born Sally Ashton, and before my husband, an Ashton had never sprung from his ancient Sicilian family root, Ashton a post-WWII invention, a dry salvation. A literary creation with only two British (sounding) syllables. The foist adopted by his entire Italian (American) clan, around 20 wops, front to back, brother to sister, wives, children born and unborn, immigrant parents gracefully dead when Salvatore switched to Alfred, Francesca to Frances, Giuseppe to Joe. Etc. What was in the new name, a sweetness? A desirable anglo-tone. Dissolving in. To. Invisibility. Having learned profoundly, it is the sounding that solidifies sense. Each put on the Ashton, the unspeakable surname already vanished like a boat at the horizon, the last boat home.

To my other self whom I originally chose not to represent

Some days and your hands are empty, as if they had no use.

Life gets lived in the imagination and all the tea rests at the bottom of the sea.

Dark days, light days, a game children play under passing cloud.

The trick: don't get caught in the open when cloud covers the sun.

Be home free.

Crimes committed against the imagination are a consequence of madness.

You've become a stranger, dumpster diving in each day hoping for a chicken to roast.

Other times you simply wait for the wash to finish.

This is one reason it took your whole life to discover constellations are configured differently elsewhere.

Now, one must exaggerate; one must endure periods of Mercury retrograde when your head is like a helium balloon.

Strange things happen either way.

Are you willing to abandon an unfortunate camp, a place of fevers, fleas, bitter water where luck runs out with the coffee and flour?

To be ambushed by words and by waiting, *flechas y fuego*.

Sometimes, truly, I say I never knew you.

Then the camera lens falls open on our missing daughter.

We are forever facing fire, the arrows.

Some days and our hands are full . . . the days come and go just the same.

Banjo Player's Daughter

The plink, the pluck, the five-string strum struck the chords the dangedy-dang twang charge, the riff so swift his fingers ring and race, know their place to bring the tune, plectrum, picks on, strafe and strike and fill the room entrancing, she dances, skips in circles in time that bridge the time, the tune melodious, mellifluous, she trips and slides, hops her shoes rise and clop the floor her father taps with his own large shoe and so the music flows, sad fifth string drone to keep the time, the beat in her bones and the joy of jiving to the tunes that no one hears now, her father gone, the banjo jangle still alive, a rising tone.

Reasons More Terrible Than Tigers
- J. L. Borges

I reeled a catfish from the river, swung it into our small boat, grabbed it, gray, slick, the gill rough on my hand. Grandpa said take the hook from its mouth and as I did the little fish bit down, caught the flesh of my finger. Blood dripped. The fish flipped and thumped in the boat's bottom, blood on my shoes. Grandpa reaching, slow motion, threw the fish back. It rose in an arc. Brown river swallowed it entirely. I watched Grandpa bandage my finger, water slapping the boat, the shore so silent and thin.

Somewhere below, a fish with a wounded mouth swims. Grandpa says fish see your shadow; I keep mine in the boat, sip cocoa from our silver thermos, wonder if the fish is following us. At dinner I'm not hungry, headless fish fried in yellow cornmeal heaped on a platter, tails brown and curled. Grandpa chewing, pulls small bones from his mouth. Grandma clatters plates and silver, offers us fruited Jell-O, the kitchen rocking like a boat.

The Unnaming

And once I said Alice because the ones I knew were all blondes and so was I. And I too wondered! How would it be to be and never answer to sally again but know another voice, a different music? Another family whose Alice had thick wavy hair, long and wide to the waist. Alice, I said. The girl who might wander if she wanted all by herself. Alice who had her own cat. Alice who curled her hair on electric rollers held with wire clips and late at night ate sugar wafers dipped in a cup of milk. And sally would peel off like a lizard skin to step out of, leave every freckle behind, the hand me downs, plain straight hair, an unmagical thirst I had endured like someone else's spell. The dried heap of it. The dandelion dross.

It would be like getting on a train and riding alone many days, my possessions tied in a pillow case. It might be a Conestoga. It needed to be a tall Appaloosa. When I got off I would know at once, as if I had never been called away. Here I am, Alice, my long curls held under a bonnet spilling out in surprise. I had walked many days. It had been endless weeks lost at sea, the pitching waves. I never looked back. I sat in my tent made of blankets, the scent of dirt and summer and arranged my few belongings impatient with the durable earth, my family of clothes pins, the red zippered suitcase, Alice maybe an Indian who made a wise circle of rocks.

Banjo Player

My dad didn't die 25 years ago. He woke up, tied his shoes, and went to work as usual, thinking *strange dream battered me last night*. He wore an expression and his faithful heart toe-tapped *strange-dream, strange-dream*, and wouldn't stop. He worked at his desk and found the commotion amusing; *whatever it takes* he thought, getting back to business, the numbers, the forecasts. At band practice that night his banjo abandoned all restraint. Each note clamored for more. The band leader blinked. The gut-bucket player saw my dad as if for the first time, almost dropped her broom handle, and fell in love. Two weeks later they married. My dad left his job and devoted himself to music and his gut-bucket girl. He grew out his hair at last and knew he would live forever.

The Offer

Because we don't know who reads these things (or why!). And *because*. Life is short and in-ter-min-a-bly long. So. I will write a cow poem and you a sally ashton. The cows are like the sally ashtons, and the sally ashtons not unlike the cows. They too are born to some existence, pushed from one unknown to the next, bathed in blood. Helpless, we are led where we do not choose. Neither chooses. We want milk and bawl until a mouth-sized nipple rests on our tongue. We die or we succeed. Either way, cows and sally ashtons, and while bovine-success differs, so does each to each of the sally ashtons' desires. Of all these, I am the only one I know. I can speak for myself who is like unto cows and often I dream of a broad meadow to lie in, legs folded, so I may regard the full face of the simple stars. So I may breathe the ready smell of grass. And now I can't tell what it is I've written. Maybe this too is like the cows.

HBHB Family Tree
Henderson, Batchelor, Humphrey, Bussicott

You must drop down the page to find her, (it feels like) falling. She is a box. Here. A wife of. Born and married with dates to prove it: 1954 to the manner born! But she hails from Bedlingtonshire, Northumberland, between Morpeth and Blyth (I, too, once lisped) though there is some question of legitimacy. Perhaps it actually was progenitor Potts! She, Sally, is given another surname. She takes it, as I took mine. My doppelganger, she will remain faceless, born 16 days earlier, married 8 years late. Our last child born the same month, the same year, 25 days apart. We are similarly joined and parted. Post-parented. Long married. Boxes, tethered by direct lines downward, mine to my name, hers away from. Who we are. She lives my life in the UK, long fingers curl around my teacup. Mine find this blind pen. It's not enough! I forgot to wake up in her bed. I lost track of. If only I had taken that scholarship. What was I thinking living in a commune so long? We reach for our toothbrush, look in the mirror and see past our missing face into the rooms beyond each other's backs where we can never wheel around and walk into who she is.

Holding Up

Donkeys

I don't remember if this happened or not but let's say it did and you were there. A Ferris wheel stalled, cotton candy sticking to fingers & the tips of our noses. When we fell in love, I think you were giving me a piggy-back ride. Perhaps chocolate played a part. Or corndogs inked with mustard; did this happen, a flood, and all we had for the mud was snowshoes? She could tell the whole story but we've lost contact over the years. Maybe it was then we first kissed, but not tongues, the moon a sugar cookie, only a bit later, midday, a bite taken out. When you read the headlines out loud I wanted you immediately, soda fizz and all, especially when you choked over the story about the elephant trainer. This is the confusing part. She told it differently but I never trusted her, what with the mackintosh and go-go boots, for god's sake it wasn't even the sixties, and that lazy eye so you never knew, you couldn't tell where you stood with that girl. What did you say that I said that made us laugh and laugh until soda did shoot out our nostrils? It's on the tip . . . you were there, I know it, whether either of you would ever admit it. I see every detail like ten minutes ago, the smell dry leaves stain the air with, wisteria begging to bloom and I wanted you naked, all mine, I could pull your long ears, what big teeth you have, oh furry ass, we were donkeys of love bucking hard across your small bed.

O . . .!

O magic wand, ruby slippers, significant bump on the head.

Where are the wizards, the goddamn white witches, the ones who will turn the present palaver to words worth repeating three times?

O hen laying golden eggs on command.

Lay, Chicken, lay!

Cruel step-mother, evil twin, false brother. Wolf hiding in granny's bed. O dusky deathsleep of the spellbound.

Enough, enough. What more can we endure?

Ducky Lucky, Cocky Locky, Sally Wally. Is the sky falling?

Quick go tell the King!

(He's in the counting house, Foxy Loxy whispers)

O lost elven ring, forgotten incantation, magic bean thrown out the window in dismay.

Crop up overnight thick as a tree towering out of this fallow to a watered land peopled with giants.

(fee-fi-fo-fum)

O, apical meristem, O rocketship to Mars . . . O, concussion!

Ending in Another Year

I've been writing this all year.

No one I knew was dying, everyone was.

Who didn't need saving?

It started in September, so much to dismantle, pack in boxes.

Or was that the dream part, the season of goodbyes?

My daughter, the last son, even the cat.

What couldn't be counted.

What couldn't be mourned.

What couldn't be remembered.

What wouldn't be forgotten.

Let's blame the cat how she lost her ninth life.

She should have kept it.

Or how the earth kept spinning and I wasn't allowed to mention it.

How death passed beside me; how I kept it busy for months.

Desiderata

Laundry might be the last act you perform on earth. Looking for the can of tuna you know is somewhere in the pantry might be the last thing you do. You select the correct water level and temperature, measure detergent, stuff in the clothes, turn the machine on and, pop!, you're done instead. Clean laundry is a good thing but make it your last thing and what good is it then? No one eulogizes laundry day, choice of soap, how well you balanced the load, or sorted, or pre-treated stains. Is it wash and wear? Not if you're dead it isn't. It won't even make it to the dryer. Dead people don't wash clothes. Dead people won't wear them for long; dead people don't eat tuna.

Le Lavandou

-a small town, France

Due to cemeteries full to bursting the mayor here bans dying and the locals obey, put off mortality until it can be accommodated, though one homeless fellow with unknown loyalties transgresses the new edict, flat out dies, and continues homeless until arrangements can be found, not easy in this seaside Mediterranean town where with rank civility the population waits for their mayor to locate a suitable plot, "not an impersonal pigeonhole."

For now the honest townspeople must remain alive: the shopkeeper watching his wife, and the woman who sells dried herbs from her stall, the dark-eyed boy in the square kicking a soccer ball, his beautiful sister kissing in an upstairs room. Her lover will wait too, and the old man who feeds pigeons then dozes in the sun, birds pecking at his shoes. The mayor, satisfied at his repeal and the cooperation of his constituency, lifts his glasses, rubs his eyes. He folds up the useless town map and goes home for lunch, a small glass of wine, a well-deserved nap before visiting the hospital. Even now his son rouses from his coma, feels hungry, rings the buzzer for the nurse. He wonders at the sound of running in the halls, how quickly the nurse appears. He asks for soup, *s'il vous plaît?*

Orison, When Nobody Looks

"We now know that the moon is demonstrably not there when nobody looks" N. David
Mermin, Physicist

Such are the repetitions of love, small as an eyelash, as inelegant as breath.

I lost my 34th year. I found lovely blue ink.

Looking out through space my eyes are not so strong.

I must see with my ears.

Cows on a hillside in some holy trinity stand in the light of the white-hearted
moon.

When someone asks what will become of us I recall, or I forget, or mainly I never
knew or smelled or touched or tasted. Tottered on. Teetered over.

Perhaps glasses allow better vision.

Perhaps there is no correction for dreams, but you do see the pines more clearly.

This could be the nightmare that ends the book.

To see better, get out the saw and hammer—build stilts.

—or embrace the sublime, horror gives way to relief.

The site of incision and blood, gaping skin. A yellowed, festered infection.

The sublime! The sublime!

To see the moon, very simple, very plain.

It's all so black and white.

What is possible in a life half the time dismantling.

What is possible after so much rain, I cannot finish here.

What is sure: the moon cannot escape its unnoted absence.

O, show yourself above our thin horizon. !

(in this same way, many once sought comfort in god)

Lunch With the Famous Poet

And after we'd finished the bread, the wine,
the plates of ravioli in brown butter sage sauce
and I had smiled through his stories and he'd
politely answered my questions about getting
published (he didn't like my manuscript's title)
there was a strange pause before he asked, carefully,
whether there was a Foot Locker shoe store in town,
and I'd answered carefully yes and he'd explained how a cat
at the house where he'd stayed the night before flying here
had peed in his shoes, his only pair, and I'd understood
he was wearing them right then, they were under our table
near mine so I'd agreed to take him shopping before the reading
to Foot Locker where he chose optic white athletic shoes
to wear with his brown pants and dim rumpled jacket—
I did point out a dark pair—but no, he preferred white
though he said he wasn't quite sure whether these fit
right and then stood as my sons once stood, hands
hanging, staring at his feet. So what else but to kneel
and press my practiced thumb into the toe of the new
size 13 ½ shoe he would wear onstage later that night?

After that I knew I'd learned a lot about poets and
the art of the business. I did change my manuscript's title
which I've just remembered was called *Don't Look Down*.
He'd said it made him want to. Look down.

And I

Highway 1 cut straight across farmland tied in place by rows of artichoke plants and I knew something was going to happen by the way the fields waited, but only a small rise in the road, and a row of pelicans flew over like single notes played on the piano, one rise led to another and just before the sea the 100,000 flipped on the odometer, the zeros lined up like a jackpot.

The Beatles were playing and I pulled over on gravel, jumped out, kissed the hood, whooped twice, hands raised, and got back in, driving. The sea on my right spun sunlight and I know it was bad, I texted my son but he sent right back. A seabird rode an updraft, who could name it? Kelp beds swayed on one side, on the other, a Hereford with a muddied face looked up and I took a bite from the apple I'd packed, the ocean called up all its blue, wave, wave, and I couldn't look over my shoulder, I was driving, there was no stopping, everything turning—the road, the CD, the astonished odometer.

Renaming Wonder

World gets chance to name new 7 wonders

What are the new seven wonders, a wren
in a hedge, a hummingbird's red-feathered throat,
wild elk that return to bugle at night

on the outskirts of some improbable city?
All that remains of the original marvels:
a vast museum of unnoticed things.

We'll never see the Hanging Gardens,
never touch the Colossus of Rhodes.
The statue of Zeus, the Temple of Artemis—

only the Great Pyramid endures.
Look for an adjective. Look
for all the clues, the bloodstains, the footprints,

the fields that weep.
Once I picked figures from clouds; now
I must memorize the heavy elements.

The heaviest will guide movement,
DaVinci wrote. Like dream,
wonder reduces to elemental dust, stories

that are a little bit prayer, a little bit
captured beetle pinned to a velvet board,
a little of what waits to be named.

Colored Orange

In the face of heightened risk, I make preparations.

I stand with my candle, a silent vigil on a bridge under baffling stars.

Without a gun, how many gallons of water are enough?

A thick, brambled hedge silhouettes against a dream's night sky. An owl perches in the upper branches.

I recall the two weeks when I was completely happy though I can't remember exactly why.

My children must be given emergency contact numbers; my mother wants to know what we would do.

How proud I am to have an owl on the property but almost as suddenly, it dives into the hedge and appears to be a small dog or large rat.

Without a gun, how much cash should I keep on hand?

A cumulus cloud inflates beyond the hilltop, a momentary country whose citizens I never get to see.

With a sputter of wax and sooty smoke the candle's flame gutters out.

The arrow has been placed on the bow; the president is to be beaten with a shoe; my husband buys seedlings for the garden.

It's as if I work all day directing traffic that isn't there.

While I don't have a gun, I keep extra candles and plenty of matches in the drawer.

But an owl, on the whole, seems a good omen.

On the Veranda

Gunshots sound nearby
who's shooting I ask
just as you say who's
running and we laugh
repeat our joke black
and white skins muted
in twilight because
how else can we
will we should we
dare we continue to talk
the night listening hard?

October 18 in the train all jumpish

A double seat to myself, but on the left side, not near the water. We could pick up more passengers. Colors not quite peak. But brilliant especially against dim sky, the river slate dimpled with messages from home. A man sits on a stump in a stump-colored jacket and watches us pass. A green pond with gray bracken: with gold leaves: with cattails burst open. The muddied bank slow and low waiting for winter. Boat clubs, fishing shacks. Boarded up buildings. Hudson, New York the next stop. Life lives before and after us: electrical towers, the telephone poles, the telephone poles, streaking wires, the insulator caps. Mud ducks, mud ducks. Autumn's bold attempt. The train runs slow. The great bridge won't collapse. Which bridge, which lives, which now? Before or after us? The Hudson seamless except where boats plow its surface. The tugboats, the dredge. A sailboat rests at anchor, sky and river both matte gray. The further bank darkens but the water glitters then flattens cement and iron. Sky turns to paper on which nothing is written that can remain or be erased. The train's whistle hollows when the banks draw closer, and the river scrambles to forget us. As if it could, braided with bridges. As if it could.

These Indian woods with a brilliance like forgetting. Wristwatch, wedding ring, shape of a shoulder hardened to a purpose. A man on the dock with a line in the water. At last the sun finds its way undercloud bringing sharp shadows, bristling the waters, the windows, any metallic thing. The river resists as if it were frozen but the sky understands the motion. What matters? The blue-windowed factory, all the right angles, brick and batten. The Thursday edition of the paper. A plethora of black coats and silver cell phones. The water's unopened envelope. Lights falling from the bridge.

Diurnal

The sun performs its declensions, the moon
its hyperbolic despair. The stars, reclusive,

appear in silence, falter one by one,
tarnished buttons lost from a dark jacket

my father once wore and a similar smell,
a quiet wool shaped by smoke. He shouldered it

in rain's coherency and against weighty night,
keys kept in one pocket, a stick of spearmint gum.

But that was years ago.

Like him the world goes on about its mysteries
unraveling a season at a time,

and what can be known of happiness turns up in a pocket
forgotten, some small, extravagant surprise.

Advent

The weekend before Thanksgiving and the Salvation Army bell ringer works the exit at the SPD market. I hear her before I see her, before I see the red bucket hanging beside her. *We need to get going early this year* she explains. I nod, smile, but don't stop. I carry one bag. It holds a bottle of vermouth, one of olive oil, a bag of organic frozen blueberries, a new toothbrush for sensitive teeth, and the holiday issue of my favorite women's magazine. In the car, bookends made from petrified bogwood, my first Christmas purchase. Also thank-you cards for recent birthday gift-givers, and eight green candles for Thanksgiving dinner. I add my sack of groceries, get in, drive.

When I get home it seems I have hit a bat. I don't know how but it huddles panting on the drive outside the garage where I've just parked my car. It's the color of mink with black ears and wings, and it turns its head to the side to eye me when I bend close. I try to speak in a bat-encouraging tone. I want to swaddle it against the dropping temperature but fear being bitten, rabies, and making its apparent fibrillation worse. It will die. I know it. Wing knuckles folded up by its ears look like a sleeping infant's fists.

Nearing Solstice

Persimmons shiver in the empty silver of branches
shaken by the weight of three blue black coal
backed rooks humping from limb to limb, their balance
caught with outspread wings unfolded until steadied
gouging beak reckless in persimmons. Copper
and coral and coal candied from every limb
veined against the sky and the ebony flash
of feather sleek bodies bend the branches thrashed,
bouncing. The fruit doesn't fall, hangs ready for no one
but crows. Gleeful cawing. Another swoops down,
another to the sound. To the color of bittersweet,
the air bitter, the persimmon sweet, overblown.
Ink of crow writing through the tree
scribing autumn, winter coming. Eat.

For A Moment

In which we pronounce joy like a word of our own.
–Wallace Stevens

Yes. There are too many things. I drive
all day, read my horoscope when I get home
that says stay home, you're too distracted

to drive today. You stand on a faraway bridge
watching the first snow in Brooklyn, your breath
bright clouds, a cell phone in one gloved hand.

The snow isn't sticking, you say.
The bridge, the river, a sky gray
and close. Small warm flakes, more like rain

dropping but the phone hot on my cheek.
You must be getting wet, love,
standing where you are, speaking

marvel to marvel, the sun here
January brilliant, nearly blinding
and the supple pause before the next goodbye.

The phone snaps, closes your side of the moon
darkened already, muffled in distance. Words
reconfigure, rustle like paper

and things never unlearned, of luck,
the smell, the first snowfall in Brooklyn,
an ache for something more.

Even a Turkey Vulture

The dog stays close at sunset and barks at every report. I tell her *good dog*. I say *squirrel!* and she races to the back fence barking and comes back grinning breathless. The crows who have stalked the blue jays' nest all afternoon now worry the vultures returning to roost—20-odd vie for a branch somewhere within three ancient eucalyptus. The jay perches on the back of a lounge chair to preen before disappearing in the cypress for the night. Which bird should I favor—vulture, crow, or jay this absurd April evening, warm as July? Soon the dog will eat strawberries the minute they blush. Soon mosquitoes will make me miserable and the vulture flock will debark for summer grounds. All the young turned from their nests. Even mine. A final vulture glides in high from the west, circles wide to slow and descend, wing tips leaning on the current, circling down now overhead, dips when I call and wave, then, to the dismay of one last crow, lands in the eucalyptus with a flap, the sound of sheets snapping on a clothesline. The jay, no longer blue but the color of night sits on a nearby branch. And what's left of the day heaves up from earth—scent, silence, and disbelief—and settles back to swiftly cooling night with all its unanswered questions. In the wisteria the fat black bee's still abuzz, and see, even a wren works the ground beneath the feeder in the light's last twinge. This is what is given. I look as long as I can see. And stars! A tablecloth pulled around my shoulders.

April Occurrences

I want to bury my face in a field of alfalfa, but I don't stop the car.

A rare white colt born in Kentucky makes the evening news.

A big-rig jack-knifes blocking the freeway during morning commute.

People wonder about poetry. A little.

The mockingbirds return.

Bears wake up, tear garbage out of dumpsters.

The 8th grade visits Washington DC and poses for pictures at the Lincoln Memorial, the Smithsonian Air and Space Museum, and Hooters Restaurant.

At least one hundred insects splatter my windshield.

Two cars spin in each other's arms. A third, unable to stop, arcs over, hits the embankment, comes to rest on its roof.

Comet Ikeya-Zhang is viewed with the naked eye.

The valley greens right up the flanks of the hills.

The air smells like syrup.

A gardener unearths a shovelful of baby moles, pink and naked, and keeps digging.

Goldfinches fight at the bird feeder.

An 8th grader pays ten dollars for a Rolex knock-off from a DC street vendor.

I roll down my window to at least smell the alfalfa better.

April surrenders to May.

Holding Up

Here at this picnic table where someone once carved the initials "*RF*" with a pocket knife—where countless hot dogs have been eaten or rolled off their buns and fallen in the dirt, a table on which jays have strutted, pecked and shat, that winter has smothered in snow, and rain has soaked relentlessly, where pine, fir, manzanita and cedar stand watch, and the ticks and clicks, buzz, warble, whistle, trills, tremolos, chirp and yat-yat-yat are the engines of another morning in which I sit, laptop open, and find internet access—the rough planks are holding up well.

Lizard

The gray-brown lizard so handsomely marked appears on a speckled rock, a movement out from shadow. Flash—freeze. Hot—cold. What the fuck are you doing here he asks the lady in the bathing suit. She sits on another rock nearby but can't hear him. He one-eyes her. And what you looking at? The absurd woman studies him, his poise and pose, then gazes again at the river cut deep in its gorge among boulders. Sparse brush and oak. Blue span above. The rush and tumble of it. Her wet bathing suit. The lizard squats, thin fingers splayed on a rock. He too stares. Into distances. For a long time. The water's roar. A suspended light. He cocks his head and licks something from the rock. I love my life he says.

This Lonesome

Time to put off the hair-shirt. Time to wash tar clumps from the scalp—floss locust legs from between the teeth and gargle forcefully with gin until the last taste of old honey expires. One horizon bursts open (this is morning), the other drains all the blood from the end of the day. Where the action is, ping-ponging between the two wearing an acrobat's suit. Self-flagellation so last-year; find someone else to despise.

Some TV show will spell everything out. In the meantime, stay out of wildernesses. In the meantime you live on a planet, a galactic dust-bunny collecting itself with each spin, perhaps wearing a bit thin at the temples, and the Minotaur can't be kept chained forever, and what there is of gladness must not be squandered, O reckless heart.

How To

Don't waste a feeling. Or a story. Or a way or worry. A minute. A birdsong. Not even one shade of green. Promise the crows anything. Remember the turkey vultures, how all spring they return one by one at dusk to roost in the eucalyptus trees. Also consider the privet that readies new berries so the seasons will continue outside the window. Write a *Carte Geographique de la Lune*—nothing more sublime can be written in English nor more shadowed with desire, nor more unsayable. That it has not been said enough, even water mouths its lonely syllable. It stutters across the sea and lays cool hands over a lake. Don't mention it anymore someone will tell you. But how can you compress the horizon or keep it from its risings? It will leer or loom or drift, a silver eyelash, a miniscule crack, an irresistible opening you long to enter. What else is there to know? So much spills out and over. And the ceiling fan spins slow. The spider in its corner spins a secret and the atoms in every part of everything spin, spin the little wheels of our hearts, spin beauty and its waning, the spider's finely wrought bundle silent, wound with silken thread.

Dedications/Notes

"Litany" (p. 32) is for Kelsea Habecker

"Sally Ashton. Controller." (p. 52) is for Sally Ashton, fiction writer, UK

"Sally Ashton (b. ca. 1845) Keswick, Va." (p. 56), as found via *Google*.

flechas y fuego (p. 58) : arrows and fire, from "Poetry," by Pablo Neruda.

"The Offer" (p. 64) is for Nin Andrews

"HBHB Family Tree" (p. 65) is for Sally Ashton, Henderson lineage, UK

"On the Veranda" (p. 81) is for Ethelbert Miller

"For A Moment" (p. 86) is for Susannah Ashton

"How To" (p. 93) is in memory of Pat O'Laughlin

Sally Ashton is a poet, writer and editor of the *DMQ Review*, an online journal featuring poetry and art. She is author of *These Metallic Days*, and the prose poem collection, *Her Name Is Juanita*. Poems also appear in *An Introduction to the Prose Poem* and *Breathe: 101 Contemporary Odes* as well as journals such as *Sentence: A Journal of Prose Poetics*, *5am*, *Mississippi Review* and *Poet Lore*. She is the recipient of an Artist Fellowship, Poetry, from Arts Council Silicon Valley and has been nominated three times for the Pushcart Prize. Ashton earned her MFA at Bennington Writing Seminars. Besides workshops, she teaches creative writing at San José State University and lives in Los Gatos, California. She blogs at www.poetryonastick.blogspot.com

Made in the USA
Charleston, SC
03 February 2010